THE WESTERNS

A PICTURE QUIZ BOOK

John Cocchi

DOVER PUBLICATIONS, INC., NEW YORK

Preface and Acknowledgments

Probably no other type of film has been as durable as the Western. A uniquely American art form, since it reflects the pioneering of our country, the Western has taken different forms in its three quarters of a century of existence on the screen. Few films made the impact that *The Great Train Robbery* did in 1903 and fewer films have survived as long.

The appeal of the Western movie is worldwide and European moviemakers have copied the style with a great deal of success. Only a handful of Westerns are being produced in the U.S. now, but the large-scale type of outdoors action film is coming back into popularity.

While an all-inclusive look at the development of the Western movie from early silent days to the present would take a volume of monumental proportions, we hope that this quiz book has covered a lot of the highlights along the trail. We also hope that this has been accomplished in an informative and entertaining way, so that the reader might learn a fact or two as he or she brings back happy memories of Saturday matinees spent with sagebrush heroes we all remember so well.

The author hopes that the reader will get as much fun out of the book as went into its making. He would also like to thank the following for their help: Alan Barbour, Paul Becton, Eric Benson, Mrs. Rose Cocchi, Ed Connor, Homer Dickens, Morris Everett, William K. Everson, Henry Fera, Ray Gallo, Pierre Guinle, Ken Jones, Bob Lane, Leonard Maltin, Alvin H. Marill, James R. Parish, Dan Scapperotti, Chris Steinbrunner, Lou Valentino; and, especially, Miles Kreuger, for helping to make this book possible.

J. C.

Published in Canada by General Publishing Company, Ltd., 30 Lesmill Road, Don Mills, Toronto, Ontario.
Published in the United Kingdom by Constable and Company, Ltd., 10 Orange Street, London WC 2.

The Westerns: A Picture Quiz Book is a new work, first published by Dover Publications, Inc., in 1976.

International Standard Book Number: 0-486-23288-3

Manufactured in the United States of America
Dover Publications, Inc.
180 Varick Street
New York, N.Y. 10014

The Silents

1–16

1. Generally regarded as the first Western, which it wasn't, and the first narrative film (again no), *The Great Train Robbery,* filmed in New Jersey in 1903, did have the very first Western star in the cast, pictured here (center) in one of his several roles. Who was he and who directed?

2. Now that we know who the first Western star was, what was his real name, and was he a real cowboy? His last film was made 62 years after his first. What was it?

The Silents

continued

3. One of the first serials was actually a series of shorts with the same characters, several of the episodes taking place in the far West. What was it and who played the heroine?

4. One of the popular stars in the Teens, seen here (plaid shirt) in *Deuce Duncan* (Triangle, 1918), was a Universal star in the Twenties and ended his career doing bits and extra work at the latter studio until a few years before his death in 1949. His name?

5. Seen here in *Don Quickshot of the Rio Grande* (Universal, 1923) is a cowboy who made few sound films. Name him.

6. The most popular cowboy star of the silents, Tom Mix worked for which studio in the Twenties? He's shown in one of their films, *Eyes of the Forest* (1923). Name his famous horse.

7. Epic Westerns were given a boost when John Ford made a sweeping saga of the linking of the Central and Union Pacific Railroads. What was it called and who were the young stars?

8. The lipsticked hero (yes, hero) on the left starred in B oaters in the Twenties and Thirties, before becoming a character actor. What was his name?

9. A popular player of the Twenties, he was on the verge of major stardom when Paramount cast him as *Jesse James* (1927). A premature death ended his career. Who was he and what was his horse's name?

10. William S. Hart's last starring film, made for United Artists in 1925, had a one-word title. What was it and why was its sound reissue unique?

11. Some cowboy stars had names like Buffalo Bill, Jr., and Wally Wales. The stalwart here was called — ?

12. Zane Grey's stories were the source of many features, some remade several times. *Code of the West* (Paramount, 1925) had two stars whose brothers and sisters were also performers. Their names?

13. The famous actor, here in another Zane Grey – Paramount feature, *Man of the Forest* (1926), had a son and daughter who later starred in Westerns. Name the three.

14. Samuel Goldwyn's production of *The Winning of Barbara Worth* (United Artists, 1926), by well-known Western author Harold Bell Wright, had two later Oscar-winning actors in leads. Name them and the director.

15. Comedy-maker Hal Roach produced several noncomic Westerns in the Twenties, one being *No Man's Law* (Pathé, 1927), which starred Rex, the King of Wild Horses. Can you name the three human actors, one of whom was on the threshold of a long career as a successful comic?

16. *The Water Hole* (Paramount, 1928), another Zane Grey special, had color scenes, our old friend from other films and a young leading lady soon to become a very popular star of early talkies. Who is she?

The Thirties

17–26

17. An already established star who was to specialize in sound Westerns and a newcomer who would eventually support every top actress at a major studio are in the midst of a sticky situation from *Fair Warning* (Fox, 1931). Identify them.

18. *Lasca of the Rio Grande* (Universal, 1931) was the title of this oater opus. Who were the leads?

The Thirties

continued

19. A threesome from *The Painted Desert* (RKO, 1931). She was a star of early sound pix, while the men were an established character actor—one of John Ford's stock company—and a not yet major star. The three?

20. Zane Grey again, this time a scene from *To The Last Man* (Paramount, 1933). One of the villains was more at home as a gangster, while the young hero was a man whom we'll be hearing more from as we read on. Their names, please.

21. An almost classic pose of hero, frightened heroine and cowering villain from one of the many B westerns of the decade, *Honor of the Range* (Universal, 1934). The star had been extremely popular in silents. The three?

22. More Zane Grey. *Home on the Range* (Paramount, 1935) had a later Oscar winner (Best Supporting Actor of 1949) being covered by a silent-screen beauty. Identify.

23. Buck Jones, famed for both silent and sound Westerns, encountered insane John Bleifer in an offbeat series entry, *The Crimson Trail* (Universal, 1935). The girl was the sister of a famous actress. Who was she? In real life, Buck died a hero's death. Elaborate.

24. The Indian taking the oath in yet another Zane Grey story, *Desert Gold* (Paramount, 1936), had a variety of famous roles for which he is known. His name?

25. A famous American actor (left) journeyed outside the country to make an early non-U.S.-filmed Western, *Silent Barriers* (Gaumont British, 1937). Can you guess the locale and the actor's name? The female lead later came to Hollywood with her actor husband and had an international career. What about her name?

26. When there were two heroes in a Western fighting over the same girl, one (the lesser of the two stars) usually got killed. Cecil B. DeMille used this formula in his *Union Pacific* (Paramount, 1939). Who were the rivals, the girl they loved and the villain who seems about to kill the wrong man?

27. A dangerous train stunt helped start off the Forties in a Universal film based on the notorious Dalton gang. What was it called: *The Daltons Ride Again, The Dalton Gang, Jesse James vs. the Daltons* or *When the Daltons Rode?*

28. MGM's epic *Northwest Passage* (1940) starred Spencer Tracy as what historical character? Which of Tracy's co-stars is pictured?

29. Here in *Viva Cisco Kid* (20th Century-Fox, 1940) are two of the many pairs of actors who portrayed Cisco and sidekick Pancho. Which two are these?

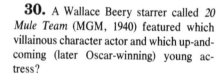

30. A Wallace Beery starrer called *20 Mule Team* (MGM, 1940) featured which villainous character actor and which up-and-coming (later Oscar-winning) young actress?

31. The popular Randolph Scott played opposite an actress who had previously made her film debut in a Western sequel. Here she played a famous Western outlaw queen. What was her name and the title of this film?

32. Wallace Beery, seen here in the flesh, played the title role in this 1941 MGM picture. Was it *Viva Villa, The Bad Man, Bad Bascomb* or *Big Jack?* Who are the other actors?

33. Howard Hughes's *The Outlaw* (1943) ran into censorship problems and was not released until 1950. Here are the four leads, including the two young stars in their film debuts. Name them and the real-life parts played by the three men.

34. A popular star of silents and Thirties films was co-starred in *Buckskin Frontier* (UA, 1943) with the leading lady of a famed TV series of the 1950s. Name them.

35. These two famed stars of silent Westerns teamed up in a Forties series for Monogram. What was it called?

36. Western duels are usually fought with sixguns, but this picture had a sword-fight. Albert Dekker and David Bruce participated in the swordplay, but the stars and the title remain to be identified.

37. *California* was a large-scale Paramount pic of 1946 which starred Ray Milland, here being held at gunpoint, and what famous female star? Can you name the man with the gun and his seaman accomplice?

38. Republic's *Wyoming* (1947) starred William Elliott and the three pictured here. Only one of the trio was American-born; which one?

39. Robert Wise's *Blood on the Moon* (RKO, 1948) had Robert Mitchum and Robert Preston (not shown) as rivals over the leading lady. Name her. Which of the leads had previously appeared in the Hopalong Cassidy series?

40. Robert Taylor's lovely leading lady in this MGM tale of the cavalry and the Indians was who? Sam Wood directed the film, which has a one-word title. Name it.

41. James Stewart starred in and Delmer Daves directed this drama which treated Indians sympathetically and helped popularize the adult Western. What was this monumental film and who co-starred as the chief?

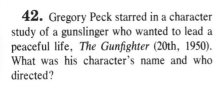

42. Gregory Peck starred in a character study of a gunslinger who wanted to lead a peaceful life, *The Gunfighter* (20th, 1950). What was his character's name and who directed?

43. Kirk Douglas' leading lady in this Howard Hawks film was an Indian model turned actress. Can you name her and the film?

44. The situation pictured here reveals the title of the film and shows the lady in question. Identify her and it.

45. James Fenimore Cooper's novels usually classified as Colonial Westerns. Which one is this 1953 Columbia film and who are the stars (the buckskin man and the lady)?

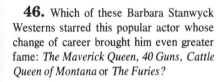

46. Which of these Barbara Stanwyck Westerns starred this popular actor whose change of career brought him even greater fame: *The Maverick Queen, 40 Guns, Cattle Queen of Montana* or *The Furies?*

47. This pretty actress, previously an Indian maiden in *Broken Arrow*, was again a redskin in *White Feather* (20th, 1955). Name her.

48. The ladies weren't spared in the action-packed Fifties, as evidenced by *Two-Gun Lady* (Associated, 1955). Can you name these opponents?

49. Frank Sinatra was a coward in this moody oater. Who was originally selected for the part of the leading lady (a famed socialite), and who finally played the role, as seen here?

50. Edward Dmytryk's offbeat Western, which starred the two actors pictured here and a third male lead, used the name of a town as its title. What was it?

The Sixties
and Seventies

51–78

51. An early Elvis Presley film cast him as a half-breed with a glamorous Thirties star as his mother. Don Siegel directed. Name the film and the actress.

52. Kirk Douglas portrayed a cowboy defeated by modern technology in this David Miller-directed feature. The blonde female star has been recognized for her considerable talents only recently. The title and the lady, please.

53. What famous foreign film inspired this 1964 MGM feature which starred Paul Newman as a Mexican bandit and Laurence Harvey as his captive?

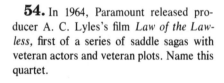

54. In 1964, Paramount released producer A. C. Lyles's film *Law of the Lawless,* first of a series of saddle sagas with veteran actors and veteran plots. Name this quartet.

55. An unsuccessful attempt to launch a new cowboy star in the mid-Sixties was undertaken by Universal. He's seen here in *Taggart* (1965). Who is he?

56. Another A. C. Lyles all-star cast was gathered for *Town Tamer* (Paramount, 1965). From left to right, they are — ?

57. Andrew V. McLaglen, directing in the style of the master—John Ford—made some comedy Westerns in the Sixties and some more serious. James Stewart squared off with what villain in which film? Look closely and you'll recognize the leading lady.

58. *Frontier Hellcat* (Columbia, 1966) was one of a slew of foreign-made Westerns, in this case German, which dominated the American market in the Sixties. Pierre Brice was the Indian Winnetou. Name the other two stars and the male lead's character name, a part he played several times.

59. *Gunpoint* (Universal, 1966) was one of the last starring Westerns of this boyish star who died in a plane crash five years later. His first claim to fame was what?

60. More A. C. Lyles, this time from a film called *Waco* (Paramount, 1966). The actor died two years later, a fate which befell quite a few of the actors in the Lyles films, while the female lead had first made her mark in another Western. Name them.

61. Last of the Lyleses. This trio from *Red Tomahawk,* one of the last of the A. C. Lyles productions for Paramount (1967), consisted of a popular leading man in the Fifties, a singer and an Academy Award winner. Who are they?

62. Englishman J. Lee Thompson directed an all-star cast in one of the last major oaters of the Sixties. Who are these two unlikely Western types?

63. Prehistoric monsters clashed with cowboys in this science-fiction Western. Name it.

64. Richard Harris portrayed a white man who becomes a member of an Indian tribe in which film of 1970?

65. A former featured villain turned international star and a famous Indian actor were in this Jim Brown-starring film for National General in 1970. Name it and the Indian actor's most famous recent role.

66. These two stars emoted in a Western made in an unusual foreign country. Called *Madron* (Four Star Excelsior, 1971), it had an Academy Award-nominated song. Can you name it, the country of origin and why the love between the two stars was impossible?

67. *Easy Rider* director-star Dennis Hopper (man in white hat) directed himself in a film about the making of a Western. What was it called and what director, shown here with the cigar, played the director of the movie-within-the-movie?

68. *Easy Rider* co-star Peter Fonda (left) made his directorial debut with this 1971 Universal Western. What was it called and who was his bearded companion?

69. Portraying brothers and villains who menaced Raquel Welch as *Hannie Caulder* (Paramount, 1972) were a formidable trio of actors. Who were they?

70. *Companeros* was a Spanish-made Western released here by the short-lived GSF Company in 1972. Its spaced-out villain was played by what master of menace?

71. A black-accented Western was directed by one of its stars. Which one, and what was the film's name?

72. James Coburn and Rod Steiger starred in this Italian-made oater for United Artists in 1972. It had two titles: can you name either one?

73. Cliff Robertson wrote, produced, directed and starred in a very personal feature which was part of a short rodeo-film cycle. Name it and at least one other film in the cycle.

74. The star of the "Stranger" series took time off to do a violence- and sex-filled Western. Name him and the title.

75. The stars of a youth-oriented Western called *Bad Company* (Paramount, 1972) were — ?

76. What well-known black athlete turned actor starred in two Westerns about a slave who became a legend in the old West?

77. Two of the boys from *American Graffiti* and one from *Summer of '42* were underaged gunmen in *The Spikes Gang* (UA, 1974). Name them. Who played Spikes?

78. *Lovin' Molly* (Columbia, 1974) was a quiet film about a lifelong love affair between a lovin' woman and two good friends. Who were these romantic three?

Academy Awards

79–90

79. The first actor to win an Oscar for a sound movie was Warner Baxter (right), for a Western. He played a famous character created by a famous writer. One of the film's directors was Irving Cummings. Name the character, author, film, co-director and co-star, as shown.

80. The first Western to be awarded a Best Picture Oscar was the fourth film to win. Name it, the stars as shown here and the authoress of the famed novel on which the movie was based.

81. Gary Cooper's favorite male co-star won his third Academy Award as Best Supporting Actor for his portrayal of a less-than-honest judge. Name the actor, film and role (a real-life character).

82. Judy Garland introduced the first Oscar-winning song from a Western. Name the song, the film and the comedienne pictured here with Judy.

83. John Wayne did a marvelous job as an aging cavalry captain in John Ford's classic *She Wore a Yellow Ribbon* (RKO, 1949). Its one Oscar was for: Best Dramatic Score, Best Color Cinematography, Best Director or Best Actor?

84. Gary Cooper won his second Best Actor award for *High Noon* (UA, 1952), which also won Oscars for Best Editing and Best Song, plus Best Score. Who wrote the song and what cowboy actor introduced it? Who else is pictured?

85. The actor in the center won his first Oscar as Best Supporting Actor of 1952. Name him and the film. Marlon Brando is at the right. Who is the lady at the left?

86. Doris Day sang the Oscar-winning song of 1953 in this musical Western, also playing the title role. What was the song and movie? Who is seen as the cavalry officer?

87. Burl Ives had strong roles in four films of 1958, winning his Oscar as Best Supporting Actor for a large-scale Western. What was its name and which of the two other actors pictured played his son?

88. This veteran actor won the Best Supporting Actor award for 1963 in a Paul Newman starrer. Name the performer and the film.

89 & 90. Which of these two won an Academy Award as Best Actor for this Western spoof? What was the relationship between the two characters pictured?

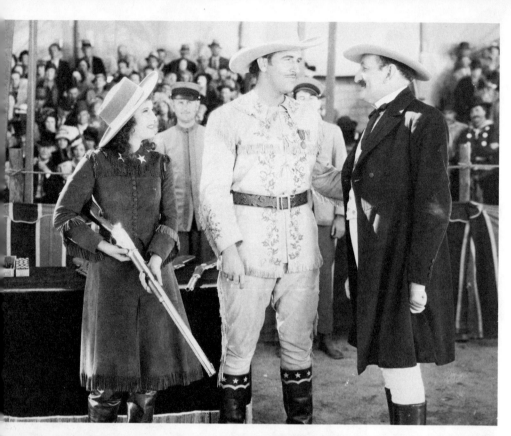

The Great Directors

91–102

91. George Stevens directed this tale of a sharpshooting lady for RKO in 1935. Who played the title role, and who was her equally dead-eyed leading man?

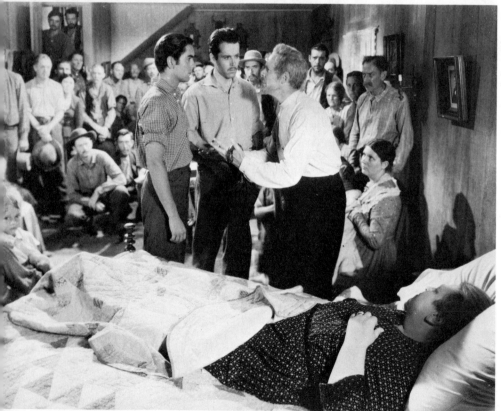

92. The James boys rode in this 1939 20th Century-Fox spectacle. Who are the men pictured in the middle, which one was Jesse and who played Frank? Can you name the director?

93. The fiery heroine was a specialty in a Cecil B. DeMille film. Who was she here? What is the name of this Gary Cooper starrer and who is being menaced by the damsel?

94. John Ford's story of the O. K. Corral starred Henry Fonda as what famous lawman? What character actress is pictured and what was the film called?

95. David O. Selznick's production of *Duel in the Sun* (1946) was directed by whom? What relationship existed between the two actors shown and what was unusual about one of the roles?

96. DeMille paired this team in a story of Colonial times. What was its name?

97. Anthony Mann directed James Stewart in eight films, seven of them in consecutive order. In which of these was Janet Leigh the leading lady? What was offbeat about the cast?

98. Who directed this epic adventure of four soldiers of fortune? Which of the four aren't pictured?

99. Ultra-violence in the West was ushered in with this now classic film of 1969, *The Wild Bunch* (Warner Bros.). Which of the two stars featured survived at the end? Who directed?

100. A climactic moment from a cult film in which the old West clashed with progress. Name the film and its director, plus its stars.

101. Name the director and the title-role stars of this feature. Where was it made?

102. A famed legend was debunked in violent fashion in this 1973 MGM release from Sam Peckinpah. The two actors played the title roles; name them and the film.

John Wayne

103–116

103. John Wayne's longevity as a Western star is evidenced by this still from his first starring film, made in 1930. Can you name it? Who directed, and why did the film fail to make Wayne a major star right away?

104. In this scene from an early series film, *Randy Rides Alone* (Monogram, 1934), Wayne battles a top stunt man who later became an Academy Award-winning second unit director. Can you name him and any other company for which Wayne starred in oaters?

105. Before *Stagecoach* made him a star, Wayne was appearing in a B series at Republic. Can you name the series and his two co-stars? The action shown here was staged for *Three Texas Steers* (1939).

106. John Ford's *Stagecoach* (UA, 1939) established Wayne as a star. What was his character name and who was his leading lady? Which of the actors pictured won an Oscar for the film?

107. *The Spoilers* (Universal, 1942) co-starred Wayne with two famous people. This comedy scene featured Marietta Canty as the maid to the female lead. Can you name her and the usually heroic male co-star, here playing the villain?

108. One of Wayne's best friends was a well-known character actor who usually played the menace to Big Duke's hero. Name him. Can you identify the 1944 RKO feature from which this scene is taken (Ella Raines was the heroine)?

109. Another milestone in Wayne's career was *Angel and the Badman* (Republic, 1947). Why? Who was his pretty and ill-fated leading lady?

110. In *Red River* (UA, 1948), Wayne did something he hadn't done before; what was it? A toothless Walter Brennan co-starred in this epic saga of the Chisholm Trail, directed by whom?

111. Howard Hawks's *Rio Bravo* (1959) was a top Warners Western. Who is the villain shown here, and what famous young singer can be seen with the rifle at the window? Five other performers also had leading roles; name as many as you can.

112. Wayne starred as *Chisum* in the 1970 Warners film of that name. Who was on the receiving end of the Wayne wrath? How is the name Chisum usually spelled?

113. David Huddleston took care of a toothy problem in this 1970 National General release with a title similar to two previous Wayne pix. Name it.

114. Maureen O'Hara was Wayne's estranged wife in *Big Jake* (National General, 1971). Does anyone remember the basic plot?

115. Starring as *Cahill: United States Marshal* (Warners, 1973), Wayne had a problem with his two sons. What was it?

116. The Duke's 1975 entry is a sequel to one of his biggest films, its title the same as that of the leading character. What is it called and to which non-Western starring his leading lady has the film been compared?

Serials

117–130

117. This popular Twenties star was known as the Queen of the Western Serials. The initials on her chaps are a clue to her name.

118. This 1925 Pathé chapter play was called *Idaho*. Its star was an actor named Mahlon Hamilton. Can you identify him in the still?

119. The title of this 1932 Mascot serial is the same as the famous novel upon which it was based. Name it and as many of the silent-screen actors shown as you recognize.

120. Sid Saylor was the comedy lead, and Ken Maynard the star, of a contemporary Western serial featuring a mystery villain called The Rattler. What was it?

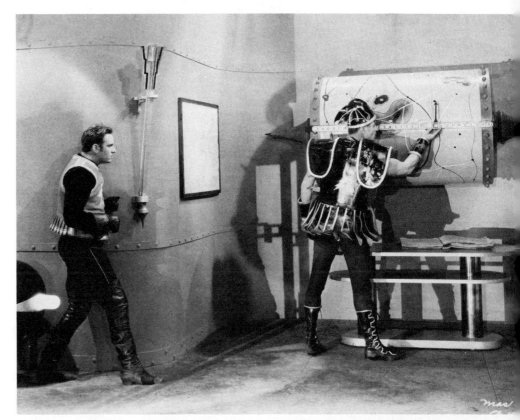

121. Yes, this was a Western serial, although it also qualified as a science-fiction musical with comedy. It helped launch a young singer on a long and successful starring career. Name the film and its lead.

122. The great Tom Mix bowed out of films in a 15-chapter serial which had something of a science-fiction plot. The title?

123. The star seen here usually wore a mask with this costume. Name him, the serial, and the author of the original story on which the character was based.

124. Name the five stars of the serial *The Lone Ranger* (Republic, 1938), three of whom underwent name changes. Which one proved to be the real Lone Ranger after the others were killed?

125. *Overland with Kit Carson* (Columbia, 1939) had a new Western star (on the left) who changed his first name after playing another historical character. What was the actor's name, before and after?

126. A comic strip inspired this 1940 Republic cliffhanger. It also gave a new name to an actor who was being built up for stardom. The names?

127. Billed as the "Million Dollar Serial" because of its cast was *Riders of Death Valley* (Universal, 1941). Identify the two actors here and as many others as you can name.

128. Robert Scott (right) starred as the Indian *Black Arrow* (Columbia, 1944). Who are his companions in the scene, one of whom was Tonto in the Lone Ranger serials?

129. *Zorro's Black Whip* (Republic, 1944) starred this pair. Name them. Which one wore the Mask?

130. One of Universal's last cliffhangers was *The Scarlet Horseman* (1946). How many of these actors look familiar?

Musicals

131–144

131. One of the first musical Westerns was Warner Bros ' *Under a Texas Moon* (1930), featuring this dancer. Was she: Movita, Acquanetta, Armida or Sabu?

132. *Under A Texas Moon* also featured this harmonizing trio, led off by George Cooper at the left. Can you name the others, one an entertainer famed for his role on stage in *Harvey* and one a popular character actor?

133. Jeanette MacDonald was *The Girl of the Golden West* in the 1938 MGM version of the David Belasco play. Nelson Eddy, of course, co-starred, but who is seen here? Who did the music?

134. Nelson Eddy appeared without Jeanette MacDonald in a Western with music and action entitled *Let Freedom Ring* (MGM, 1939). Who are the three famous character actors seen with Nelson?

135. This musical-comedy Western starred a popular comedienne who had already embarked on a long career as Blondie. The title of this 1941 Columbia film, which also starred Glenn Ford and Ann Miller, was a switch on a very famous saying. Name the actress and the film.

136. Possibly the most popular team in Western musicals was this pair, seen here in *Along the Navajo Trail* (Republic, 1945). Were they married at the time?

137. *Annie Get Your Gun* (MGM, 1950) starred this popular actress-singer-dancer. Name her, the number being performed here and the composer.

138. Bob Hope and Lucille Ball starred in this musical remake of the classic *Ruggles of Red Gap* (Paramount, 1935). Name it.

139. Using surrealistic sets, this musical satire managed to kid every Western cliché in offbeat fashion. Name this Paramount film of 1954 and its singing female lead.

140. Howard Keel and Jane Powell (center) starred in *Seven Brides for Seven Brothers* (MGM, 1954). Which of the following were not among the brothers: Keel, Matt Mattox, Russ Tamblyn, Jeff Richards, Bobby Van, Bob Fosse, Tommy Rall, Marc Platt, Jacques D'Amboise?

141. While *Seven Brides for Seven Brothers* was inspired by the Rape of the Sabine Women, a 1955 Universal film called *The Second Greatest Sex* could boast *Lysistrata* as its inspiration. That doesn't really help you to identify three of the leads, as shown here.

142. The film version of *Oklahoma!* (Magna/20th Century-Fox, 1955) was a long time in coming, the stage musical having been produced in 1943. Who finally starred on screen as Laurey and Curly? What famed team wrote the songs?

143. Who was Debbie Reynolds' leading man in this film? She had the title role in this 1964 MGM musical. Name it.

144. Clint Eastwood was one of three non-singing stars who attempted to do justice to the songs of Alan Jay Lerner and Frederick Loewe in *Paint Your Wagon* (Paramount, 1969). Who were the other two, and who directed?

Comedies

145–166

145. This popular silent star, seen here in *The Sunshine Trail* (Associated First National, 1923), later became a producer. Can you name him?

146. A Mack Sennett comedy called *Riders of the Purple Cows* (Pathé, 1924) was a takeoff, at least in name, on what famous and often-filmed novel? Can you name the actor in the middle and the comic on the right?

147. The stars of this late silent comedy, *Lightning* (Tiffany, 1927), were a leading actress and a cowboy star of both silent and sound films. Can you identify either one?

148. This beloved child star made her Western debut in a short, *The Pie-Covered Wagon* (Educational, 1932). Do you know the name of the series from which this short derives?

149. This great team is seen in which film?

150. One of the films in a very popular series found the principals in a Western setting. Can you name the boy and girl in this scene?

Comedies

continued

151. How many can you identify in this still from *The Kid from Texas* (MGM, 1939)?

152. This top comedy team made their Western debut in a Universal comedy of 1942. What was its title and which studio cowboy star appeared with them?

153. The battling twosome here, paired in three Universal Westerns of the Forties, were both from Canada. Can you name them and identify which film is depicted: *Salome, Where She Danced*, (1945), *Frontier Gal* (1945) or *River Lady* (1948)?

154. Vincent Price (not pictured) was a star of this spoof with the marvelous title *Curtain Call at Cactus Creek* (U-I, 1950), but who were the others?

155. By 1951, the Hopalong Cassidy Westerns were so popular on TV that MGM made a spoof of the craze. Give the title and the stars' names.

156. Ginger Rogers starred in the title role of this comedy which some people refer to as the movie that closed RKO Studios. Name this 1956 film and Ginger's leading man.

157. One of Bob Hope's Western spoofs was this 1959 United Artists feature. Who played the title role?

158. An unlikely trio co-starred with John Wayne in the comedy *North to Alaska* (20th, 1960). Who were they and which one can be regarded as a Western actor?

159. The title of this Debbie Reynolds starrer was also the name of a song, which was not sung in the film. What was the film called, and who are flanking her?

160. The cavalry was spoofed in George Marshall's *Advance to the Rear* (MGM, 1964). Name the four stars.

161. Henry Fonda and Glenn Ford starred in a 1965 MGM comedy as two itinerant cowboys. What was it called and who directed?

162. Another unlikely trio in an unlikely comedy, *Texas Across the River* (Universal, 1966). They should be easy to name.

Comedies

continued

163. Disney's *One Little Indian* (Buena Vista, 1973) paired which two familiar leads?

164. Slim Pickens led a raid on the town in *Blazing Saddles* (Warners, 1974), but why are the townspeople so wooden?

165. Just one of the three stars of *Don't Turn the Other Cheek!* (International Amusement, 1974) is American. Which one, and who are the others?

166. The two stars of Frank Perry's *Rancho Deluxe* (UA, 1975) are among the most popular young actors in films today. They are — ?

Remakes

167–174

167. The first sound version of this durable Rex Beach tale had which two brawlers in an epic fight?

168. *The Squaw Man* (MGM, 1931) was remade by the same director who had originally filmed it in 1914. Name him and the two actors pictured.

169. Another classic brawl, this time on the distaff side. Name the picture and Marlene Dietrich's opponent. What usually happened at the end of a Dietrich Western?

170. Can you think of the name of Robert Taylor's leading lady in this outdoor epic? The basic story has been done many times, but this was a direct remake of a 1930 MGM film of the same title. What was it called?

171. The 1942 Universal remake of this property (the fourth film version of this tale) had which silent-screen star as Marlene Dietrich's knife-wielding friend?

172. Joel McCrea had the leading role in the 1946 Paramount edition of the Owen Wister classic, later a TV series. Who was the lady, and what immortal line comes from this story?

173. Shelley Winters fought whom in a rehash of the feminine barroom brawl from *Destry Rides Again?* What was this version called?

174. *Cimarron* (MGM, 1961), a new version of the first Oscar-winning Western, co-starred Glenn Ford and what actress as Dixie Lee? What famous land rush was depicted?

The "B" Stars

175–198

175. Battling badmen is part of the job. The hero, on the right, is seen in *The Ghost Rider* (Superior, 1935). He is — ?

176. Formerly a dramatic actor, he starred in a series for Columbia in 1935–36, of which *Ranger Courage* (1936) with Martha Tibbetts is typical. His name?

177. The star of a long-running Columbia series (1935–1952), he was popular before he adopted a character portrayal which brought greater fame. He and Rosalind Keith are sharing a rare quiet moment in *Westbound Mail* (1937).

178. This singing cowboy made the musical Western a way of life, standardizing the comedy sidekick, novelty acts and film title named after a popular song. *Git Along Little Dogies* (Republic, 1937) is the film, The Maple City Four the comics. Can you name the star, his sidekick and the leading lady?

179. Known as King of the Cowboys, he eclipsed the previous musical Western star in popularity. He's seen here in *The Ranger and the Lady* (Republic, 1940), being held at gunpoint by Harry Woods and his men. The lady is Jacqueline Wells, who later changed her name. Identify the star and give the lady's better-known name.

180. Two for the price of one was the formula used for *Riders of Pasco Basin* (Universal, 1940) and many other oaters. This film teamed two stars in the leads, seen here left and right. Name them. How about the pretty leading lady?

181. A star for Monogram from 1937 to 1940, he was a singer and the brother of another Western star. He died while making a serial in 1945, suffering a fatal heart attack. The badman here in *Covered Wagon Trails* (1940) was known both as Sam, the bartender, on the *Gunsmoke* TV series, and as the Frankenstein monster.

182. The Hopalong Cassidy series was the most successful of all Western films in terms of number, 66 in all. Can you name these three from *Border Vigilantes* (Paramount, 1941) and their character parts?

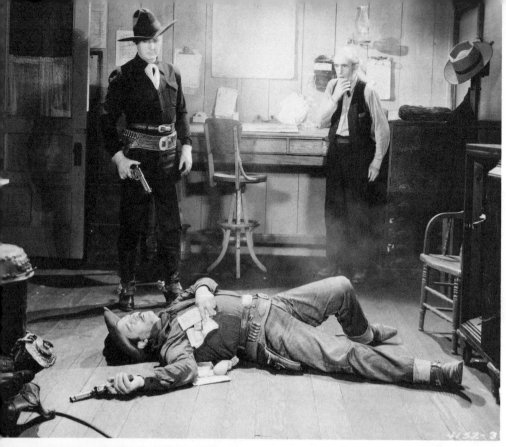

183. The winner of the gun battle was an Army colonel and an Indian expert who started in the middle Twenties and continued as a star until the early Forties. The loser in this scene from *Gunman from Bodie* (Monogram, 1941) was a very well-known Western character actor.

184. The extremely popular "Three Mesquiteers" series was constantly changing its leading men. This trio took over in such films as *Valley of Hunted Men* (Republic, 1942). The man in the middle was later a Mouseketeer, the other two were veteran cowboy actors.

185. The man with the gun was a Thirties star who made his last appearance in a leading role in Buck Jones's *Dawn on the Great Divide* (Monogram, 1942) and was married to a famed star. Harry Woods was again a villain and the lady observed here didn't do Westerns for the most part.

186. Dual roles usually meant a chance for the hero to play a bad guy and virtually every Western star had a double part at one time or another. This not-too-successful optical shot is from *The Drifter* (PRC, 1943). Name the star(s) and the outlaw role he had previously played.

187. One of the last starring Westerns for this player (left) at Republic was *Outlaws of Santa Fe* (1944), before he concentrated on straight dramas there and freelanced elsewhere. Can you name him and any of the character actors pictured?

188. The original Stony Brooke of the "Three Mesquiteers" series, this star (left) was the brother of another cowboy actor. Name the star, pictured in *Beneath Western Skies* (Republic, 1944), and brother.

189. *Rough Riders of Cheyenne* (Republic, 1945) helped boost this strumming cowboy into his own series. Who was he and who was the lanky lead?

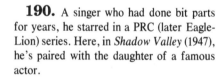

190. A singer who had done bit parts for years, he starred in a PRC (later Eagle-Lion) series. Here, in *Shadow Valley* (1947), he's paired with the daughter of a famous actor.

191. This Mexican-born actor was one of the many to play the role of The Cisco Kid. He appears here with Teala Loring, one of actress Debra Paget's sisters, in *Riding the California Trail* (Monogram, 1947).

192. A typical entry in Republic's "Red Ryder" series was *Homesteaders of Paradise Valley* (1947). Who played Red? What now-famous actor was the Indian boy, and what was the name of his character?

193. Fast with a whip, he starred for PRC and Screen Guild, here in the latter company's *Dead Man's Gold* (1948). He also has the dubious distinction of starring in one of the few (to date) sex Westerns.

194. Fast with a lash, he starred in a series with a veteran comic who should be remembered from the Hoppy films. This is from *Shadows of the West* (Monogram, 1949).

195. An RKO star before and after the war, he is seen here comforting an actress who later married Marlon Brando. His sidekick, at the right, was usually billed as Chito Rafferty and was played by Richard Martin. The film is *The Mysterious Desperado* (1949).

196. An unusual still from the Charles Starrett Western *South of Death Valley* (Columbia, 1949), in that he is seen in his masked character, fighting an actor who was famous for another masked-man role. Name the other actor and their mysterious parts.

197. Two actors who had graduated from the Hopalong Cassidy films were teamed in a series of six Lippert Westerns in 1950. The two?

198. Last of the singing cowboys, he brought an era to an end at Republic, later went on to narrating Disney films. In *Down Laredo Way* (1953), he dealt with the studio's best villain. Name them.

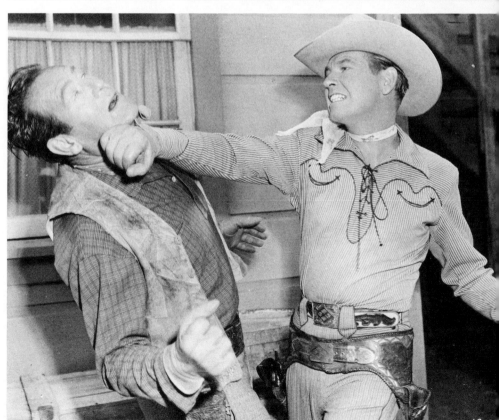

The Big Stars

199–216

199. James Cagney and Humphrey Bogart weren't at home in Westerns, making just a handful apiece. They teamed up in one for their home studio. Can you name the film and the studio? It had the same director as *42nd Street* (1933); can you name him?

200. The first of four pictures made by this team was the only Western. Name it.

201. Can you name the only Western which Katharine Hepburn and Spencer Tracy made together, the director and the veteran actor seen here with Miss Hepburn?

202. This was one of Alan Ladd's most successful starring Westerns. Name it and any of the co-stars you recognize.

203. Point out Marlene Dietrich's two leading men in this scene from a 1952 RKO Radio picture. At least one of the secondary villains should be familiar: which one? Identify the film and its German director.

204. Co-starred several times, these two top names had the leads in *The Moonlighter* (Warners, 1953), which utilized a craze of its time and had something of a distinction. What?

205. Marilyn Monroe's first lead in a Western was as Robert Mitchum's co-star in this 1954 20th Century-Fox release. Give the title, its director (a man with a reputation for being hard on actors) and the name of the other male lead.

206. Joan Crawford watched Frank Ferguson get the drop on others in this scene from *Johnny Guitar* (Republic, 1954), but with whom did she have a big showdown and who played the title role?

The Big Stars

continued

207. Which star played what historical character in *Gunfight at the O. K. Corral* (Paramount, 1957)?

208. Who directed Marlon Brando in *One-Eyed Jacks* (Paramount, 1961)?

209. Debbie Reynolds was one of the many stars of this episodic film which had three directors. What was its name?

210. An up-and-coming actress and a veteran star had leads in this Civil War story, which much later became a Broadway musical. Give the title and stars.

211. Raquel Welch was a gun-toting lady in this James Stewart – Dean Martin co-starrer. What was it called?

212. Upon returning from Europe and a successful string of spaghetti Westerns, Clint Eastwood made his U.S. starring Western debut in what feature?

213. Frank Sinatra chose to bow out of films in this comedy Western. Can you name it and his pretty leading lady, seen here as an Indian maiden?

214. This Western was certainly off-beat, as evidenced by the aftermath of a fight. Called *Red Sun* (National General, 1972), it had two international stars among its leads. Name the two here.

215. Clint Eastwood used a modernistic weapon in this oater, which was unusual in that it was neither directed by Eastwood nor rated R. Was it *The Beguiled, High Plains Drifter, Joe Kidd* or *Breezy?*

216. This Oscar-winning actress made her last film three years before her death. Can you give its name and that of its star? Why might this be considered a jinx film?

Everybody
Made Westerns

217–232

217. The "lady of the grapefruit" and a famous screen detective who also portrayed a president teamed in *Wild Brian Kent* (20th Century-Fox, 1936). Who are they?

218. *Rebellion* (Crescent, 1936) had two stars who underwent name changes. She was Rita Cansino and he started out with DeMille as George Duryea and later became Richard Powers. What were their more famous names?

219. Randolph Scott (left) certainly made a lot of Westerns. In *The Texans* (Paramount, 1938), he was teamed with an actor who later became a TV series star and a blonde beauty who became a brunette that year. The two?

220. Leading lady to Ray Corrigan and John Wayne in a "Three Mesquiteers" entry called *New Frontier* (Republic, 1939) was a new actress who later won an Oscar under another name for her "first" film. Can you give both of her screen names?

221. The only Western of this famed Thirties star was *When the Daltons Rode* (Universal, 1940). She is seen here with a character actress whom any film buff should recognize. Can you name these ladies?

222. Gene Autry's *Melody Ranch* (Republic, 1940) had a big cast which included Jimmy Durante and the three seen here, a singer-dancer, the screen's favorite sidekick and a young singer. Name them.

223. Universal's *Badlands of Dakota* (1941) had in its cast a popular comedian and an ill-fated actress whose autobiography was posthumous. She played a character modeled on Calamity Jane, but called just plain Jane. Who were they?

224. The stars of *Thunderhoof* (Columbia, 1948) were later popular on TV, he for the early comedy series *It's a Great Life* and she as "queen of the soap operas" and star of the longest-running daytime dramatic series. Their names?

225. A fluttery comedienne who had been plying her trade since silents found comfort with a popular character actor in *The Denver and Rio Grande* (Paramount, 1952). Can you name either one?

226. This popular singer made only two starring movies, both Westerns. Can you name him and his second leading lady here in *Toughest Man in Arizona* (Republic, 1952)?

227. Edward G. Robinson made a few Westerns, this one with Dianne Foster. In it he played a crippled rancher with a warped wife. Can you name the film and Robinson's co-stars?

228. The threesome in the independent *Outlaw Queen* (Globe Releasing, 1956) consisted of the actor-spokesman for the King Family, a popular Forties actress for Warner Bros. and a famous bandleader. Who are they?

229. Two of the featured leads in *Gunfight at the O. K. Corral* (Paramount, 1957) were an Academy Award-winning actress and an always-reliable actor, who were — ?

230. A country-and-western singing star played himself in *The Ballad of a Gunfighter* (Parade Pictures, 1964) and, oddly enough, got killed. His name?

1869-37

231. Leading ladies in *Heaven with a Gun* (MGM, 1969) were an up-and-coming actress and an already established player. Name them.

232. Sam Peckinpah's most gentle film, *Junior Bonner* (Cinerama, 1972), featured what director-actress as Steve McQueen's mother? Who were her other son and her husband?

Answers

*Stills **A** through **F** appear on the covers.*

A. John Wayne was Rooster Cogburn in *True Grit* (Paramount, 1969; directed by Henry Hathaway), with Kim Darby and singer Glen Campbell.

B. *Shane* (Paramount, 1953), with Alan Ladd, Jean Arthur and Van Heflin, directed by George Stevens. Loyal Griggs won for Best Cinematography; all the other awards went to *From Here to Eternity*.

C. Burt Lancaster and Jean Peters. Director: Robert Aldrich.

D. Football star Joe Namath. Director: Denys McCoy.

E. Gene Wilder and Cleavon Little stumbled from their Western set onto a neighboring set where a musical was being filmed.

F. Liv Ullmann and Gene Hackman, playing the title roles in *Zandy's Bride*. Director: Jan Troell.

1. The star was Broncho Billy Anderson; Edwin S. Porter directed for the Edison Company.

2. Broncho Billy (G. M. Anderson), seen here (center) in *Broncho Billy's Oath* (1913; directed by him), was born Max Aronson in Little Rock, Arkansas. He was never a cowboy. He bowed out in *The Bounty Killer* (Embassy, 1965).

3. The famous *Perils of Pauline* (Eclectic, 1914), starring Pearl White. Directors: Donald MacKenzie and Louis Gasnier.

4. William Desmond, shown here restraining Ed Brady from forcing himself on heroine Luella Maxim. Director: Thomas E. Heffron.

5. Jack Hoxie, with leading lady Elinor Field. Director: George Marshall.

6. Tom was a Fox (later 20th Century-Fox) star, whose trusty steed was named Tony. Director: Lambert Hillyer.

7. *The Iron Horse* (Fox, 1924), with Madge Bellamy and George O'Brien.

8. Buddy Roosevelt, circa 1925.

9. Fred Thomson, seen in *The Bandit's Baby* (FBO, 1925; directed by James P. Hogan), with the almost-human Silver King.

10. *Tumbleweeds*, reissued in 1939, featured a prologue in which William S. Hart spoke of his career, his only sound appearance. This brief segment has come to be regarded as Hart's own epitaph, delivered by himself. Director: King Baggot.

11. Bill Cody (after Buffalo Bill Cody), here in *The Galloping Cowboy* (Associated Exhibitors, 1926), with Florence Ulrich. Director: William Craft.

12. Owen Moore (brother of Tom and Matt) and Constance Bennett (sister of Joan and Barbara; father Richard also acted). Comic Eddie Gribbon is at the right. Director: William K. Howard.

13. Jack Holt, father of Tim and Jennifer. Director: John Waters.

14. Ronald Colman (left) and Gary Cooper. Henry King directed. Barbara was played by Vilma Banky, incidentally.

15. Barbara Kent, Oliver Hardy (of Laurel &, here as a villain) and Theodore Von Eltz. Director: Fred Jackman.

16. Nancy Carroll was Jack Holt's leading lady this time. Director: F. Richard Jones.

17. George O'Brien (left) and George Brent, later a popular leading man at Warner Bros. Director: Alfred E. Werker.

18. Leo Carrillo, later famed as Pancho in the "Cisco Kid" series, here literally supporting Dorothy Burgess. Johnny Mack Brown also starred in this picture. Director: Edward Laemmle.

19. The improbably named Helen Twelvetrees, J. Farrell MacDonald and a young Clark Gable. Star of the film was Bill Boyd, before he became Hopalong Cassidy. Director: Howard Higgin.

20. Jack La Rue, menacing Randolph Scott, as James Mason (not the British star) lies in danger. Director: Henry Hathaway.

21. Cecilia Parker (later Andy Hardy's sister), the star Ken Maynard, and badman supreme Fred Kohler. Director: Alan James.

22. Dean Jagger, who won an Academy Award for *Twelve O'Clock High*, here not really too worried by Evelyn Brent's automatic. Director: Arthur Jacobson.

23. Buck's leading lady was Loretta Young's sister Polly Ann. Director: Al Raboch. Jones died as a result of the Cocoanut Grove nightclub fire in Boston in 1942, after attempting to rescue some of the trapped patrons.

24. Buster Crabbe, also known as Flash Gordon, Buck Rogers, Tarzan, Billy the Kid, etc. Director: James Hogan.

25. Richard Arlen starred in this Canadian epic. Lilli Palmer (later wife of Rex Harrison) was the female lead. Director: Milton Rosmer.

26. Robert Preston, about to demise, and Joel McCrea loved Barbara Stanwyck. McCrea prevailed, despite Brian Donlevy's dirty tactics.

27. *When the Daltons Rode* (1940; directed by George Marshall). All the others were made later.

28. Tracy played Major Robert Rogers, who led a group of Colonial rangers in fighting the Indians while finding a route to the sea. Robert Young, with the notebook, also starred, as did Walter Brennan. To the left of Tracy (in profile) is Truman Bradley; to the right of Young is Donald MacBride. Director: King Vidor.

29. Cesar Romero, who had been a villain in a previous Cisco Kid movie, and Chris-Pin Martin. Director: Norman Foster.

30. Douglas Fowley and Anne Baxter. Director: Richard Thorpe.

31. Gene Tierney, who debuted in *The Return of Frank James* (20th, 1940), starred as *Belle Starr* (20th, 1941; directed by Irving Cummings) opposite Randy Scott.

32. All are Beery titles, but *The Bad Man* is correct. Also seen are Nydia Westman and Chill Wills. Directed by Richard Thorpe.

33. Thomas Mitchell (Pat Garrett), Walter Huston (Doc Holliday), Jane Russell and Jack Beutel (Billy the Kid).

34. Richard Dix, with Jane Wyatt of *Father Knows Best. Buckskin Frontier* was directed by Lesley Selander.

35. Ken Maynard and Hoot Gibson starred as "The Trail Blazers."

36. *Salome, Where She Danced* (Universal, 1945) starred Yvonne De Carlo and Rod Cameron. Director: Charles Lamont.

37. Barbara Stanwyck starred with Milland. George Coulouris held the gun and Albert Dekker looked on. Director: John Farrow.

38. John Carroll. Vera (Hruba) Ralston was Czech-born and Maria Ouspenskaya came from Russia. Director: Joseph Kane.

39. Barbara Bel Geddes was the girl, Mitchum the veteran of Hoppy films. Tom Tully is at the right.

40. Arlene Dahl, in *Ambush* (1949).

41. *Broken Arrow* (20th, 1950), with Jeff Chandler as Cochise.

42. Peck was (Jimmie) Ringo; Henry King was the director.

43. Elizabeth Threatt, in *The Big Sky* (RKO, 1952).

44. Joan Leslie, as *The Woman They Almost Lynched* (Republic, 1952). Director: Allan Dwan.

45. *The Pathfinder*, with George Montgomery and Helena Carter. Stephen Bekassy is at the left and Rodd Redwing, the famous fast-draw expert, plays the Indian. Director: Sidney Salkow.

46. (Governor) Ronald Reagan in *Cattle Queen of Montana* (RKO, 1954). Director: Allan Dwan.

47. Debra Paget. Director: Robert D. Webb.

48. Marie Windsor and Robert Lowery. Director: Richard Bartlett.

49. *Johnny Concho* (UA, 1956) saw Phyllis Kirk replacing Gloria Vanderbilt. Director: Don McGuire.

50. *Warlock* (20th, 1959), which starred a blonde Anthony Quinn and Henry Fonda, opposite Richard Widmark.

51. *Flaming Star* (20th, 1960), with Dolores Del Rio (center) and Marian Goldina.

52. *Lonely Are the Brave* (Universal, 1962); Gena Rowlands.

53. *Rashomon* (1952), the Japanese classic, was the basis for *The Outrage* (directed by Martin Ritt).

54. Dale Robertson, William Bendix, Kent Taylor and Barton MacLane. Director: William F. Claxton.

55. Tony Young. Director: R. G. Springsteen.

56. Lon Chaney, Jr., Richard Jaeckel, Dana Andrews and Richard Arlen. Director: Lesley Selander.

57. Jack Elam is the villain, Maureen O'Hara (and Chuck Hayward) behind the fence, in *The Rare Breed* (Universal, 1966).

58. Stewart Granger as Old Shatterhand and Elke Sommer. Director: Alfred Vohrer.

59. Audie Murphy, the most decorated soldier of World War II. Director: Earl Bellamy.

60. Wendell Corey and Jane Russell. Director: R. G. Springsteen.

61. Scott Brady, Howard Keel and Broderick Crawford. Director: R. G. Springsteen.

62. Julie Newmar and Omar Sharif in *Mackenna's Gold* (Columbia, 1969).

63. *The Valley of Gwangi* (Warners, 1969; directed by James O'Connolly).

64. *A Man Called Horse* (National General; directed by Elliot Silverstein).

65. Lee Van Cleef and Iron Eyes Cody in *El Condor.* Director: John Guillermin. Iron Eyes appears in the ecology TV commercial as the Indian weeping over America's garbage-strewn countryside.

66. Made in Israel, the film featured the song "Till Love Touches Your Life." Richard Boone was a gunfighter and Leslie Caron portrayed a nun. Director: Jerry Hopper.

67. *The Last Movie* (Universal, 1971) with Samuel Fuller. Other actors were Severn Darden (holding hat) and Sylvia Miles (right, back to camera).

68. *The Hired Hand,* with Warren Oates.

69. Strother Martin, Ernest Borgnine and Jack Elam. Director: Burt Kennedy.

70. Jack Palance. Director: Sergio Corbucci.

71. *Buck and the Preacher* (Columbia, 1972) starred Harry Belafonte (left) and Sidney Poitier, who also directed.

72. *Duck, You Sucker!,* later called *A Fistful of Dynamite.* Director: Sergio Leone.

73. Robertson's film was *J. W. Coop* (Columbia, 1972); others were *Junior Bonner, The Honkers, When the Legends Die* and *Black Rodeo* (a documentary).

74. Tony Anthony, here being threatened by Magda Konopka, was a blind master-gunman in *Blindman* (20th, 1972; directed by Ferdinando Baldi.)

75. Jeff Bridges and Barry Brown. Director: Robert Benton.

76. Fred Williamson, here with Tricia O'Neil, appeared in *The Legend of Nigger Charley* (Paramount, 1972; directed by Martin Goldman) and its sequel, *The Soul of Nigger Charley.*

77. Left to right: Charlie Martin Smith, Gary Grimes (he was in *Summer of '42*) and Ron Howard. Lee Marvin starred as Harry Spikes. Director: Richard Fleischer.

78. Blythe Danner, Beau Bridges and Tony Perkins. Director: Sidney Lumet.

79. Baxter played O. Henry's Cisco Kid in *In Old Arizona* (Fox, 1929), co-directed by Raoul Walsh and also starring Edmund Lowe.

80. *Cimarron* (RKO, 1931) starred Irene Dunne and Richard Dix. Edna Ferber's novel was directed by Wesley Ruggles.

81. Walter Brennan played Judge Roy Bean in *The Westerner* (Goldwyn-UA, 1940; directed by William Wyler).

82. "On the Atchison, Topeka and the Santa Fe" (by Harry Warren and Johnny Mercer) from *The Harvey Girls* (MGM, 1946; directed by George Sidney), with Virginia O'Brien.

83. Winton Hoch won for Best Color Cinematography.

84. The title song, by Dimitri Tiomkin and Ned Washington, was sung by Tex Ritter. Also starred were Katy Jurado, (Princess) Grace Kelly and Lloyd Bridges. Director: Fred Zinnemann.

85. Anthony Quinn for *Viva Zapata!* (20th, 1952). The lady is Margo. Lou Gilbert is the other actor; Elia Kazan directed.

86. Dodo introduced "Secret Love" (by Sammy Fain and Paul Francis Webster) in *Calamity Jane* (WB, 1953). Philip Carey was a handsome lieutenant, while Howard Keel played Wild Bill Hickok. Also in the still (extreme left and right) are Chubby Johnson and Benny Corbett. Director: David Butler.

87. *The Big Country* (UA, 1958; directed by William Wyler) had Chuck Connors (left) as Ives's cowardly son and Gregory Peck as the hero.

88. Melvyn Douglas, for *Hud* (Paramount, 1963; directed by Martin Ritt).

89 & 90. Surprise. Both are Lee Marvin in *Cat Ballou* (Columbia, 1965; directed by Elliot Silverstein) playing gunfighting brothers, Kid Shelleen (good) and Tim Strawn (bad).

91. Barbara Stanwyck starred as *Annie Oakley* with Preston Foster as her co-star. Melvyn Douglas was another star. The actor at the right is Theodore Lorch.

92. *Jesse James,* directed by Henry King, starred Tyrone Power (Jesse), Henry Fonda (Frank) and Henry Hull. Jane Darwell, lying on the bed, was their mother, and Lon Chaney, Jr., who can be seen over Hull's shoulder, was one of the gang. The mustached man by the wall is Harry Tyler.

93. Paulette Goddard and Lynne Overman (left) were featured with Coop in *North West Mounted Police* (Paramount, 1940).

94. Fonda (hatless, center) was Wyatt Earp in *My Darling Clementine* (20th, 1946), with Jane Darwell. Also shown are Francis Ford (far left), Harry Woods (with gun), Roy Roberts and Hank Bell (walrus mustache at right).

95. King Vidor directed; Gregory Peck and Joseph Cotten were brothers and usual good guy Peck was the bad one for a change.

96. Gary Cooper and Paulette Goddard, previously in *North West Mounted Police,* were reteamed in *Unconquered* (Paramount, 1947).

97. *The Naked Spur* (MGM, 1953) had only five actors in its cast; the others were Robert Ryan, Ralph Meeker and Millard Mitchell.

98. Richard Brooks directed *The Professionals* (Columbia, 1966), with Lee Marvin and Burt Lancaster. Also appearing as title-role characters were Robert Ryan and Woody Strode.

99. Both Ernest Borgnine and William Holden were killed off, while co-star Robert Ryan was one of the few survivors. Sam Peckinpah directed.

100. Sam Peckinpah directed *The Ballad of Cable Hogue* (Warners, 1970), with Stella Stevens and Jason Robards topcast.

101. Robert Altman directed Warren Beatty and Julie Christie as *McCabe & Mrs. Miller* on location in Canada (Vancouver, British Columbia, to be exact).

102. Singer Kris Kristofferson (Billy) and James Coburn (Pat) were less than heroic in *Pat Garrett and Billy the Kid.*

103. *The Big Trail* (Fox, 1930), directed by Raoul Walsh, was an early wide-screen film. It couldn't be shown to full advantage in many theatres and subsequently failed to do well.

104. Yakima Canutt is getting the worst of the choking. Director: Harry Fraser. Wayne also starred in Warner Bros. and Republic Westerns, did a few for Columbia and Paramount.

105. Wayne's last B series was part of the "Three Mesquiteers" features. Max Terhune, stepping on the badman at the left, and Ray "Crash" Corrigan (right) also starred. All eight of Wayne's entries were directed by George Sherman.

106. Wayne was The Ringo Kid, opposite Claire Trevor. Here, he and George Bancroft sober up the drunken doctor Thomas Mitchell (center), who won as Best Supporting Actor.

107. Marlene Dietrich and the ever-popular Randolph Scott. Director: Ray Enright.

108. Ward Bond in *Tall in the Saddle.* Director: Edwin L. Marin.

109. This was the first film produced by Wayne. Director: James Edward Grant. Gail Russell, who died of alcoholism at 36, shared billing with him.

110. Wayne aged in the film, which Howard Hawks directed. At the left is Ray Hyke, at the right are Chief Yowlachie and Hank Worden.

111. Claude Akins faced Wayne, while Ricky Nelson held his gang at bay. Also in the cast: Dean Martin, Walter Brennan, Angie Dickinson, Ward Bond and John Russell.

112. Forrest Tucker. The accepted spelling is Chisholm, as in the trail named after this cattleman. Director: Andrew V. McLaglen.

113. *Rio Lobo* (directed by Howard Hawks) was practically a remake of *Rio Bravo* (1959), but no relation to *Rio Grande* (Republic, 1950).

114. Wayne was out to retrieve his grandson from Richard Boone and his dastardly gang of kidnappers. Director: George Sherman.

115. They had been forced to help George Kennedy rob a bank. Director: Andrew V. McLaglen.

116. *Rooster Cogburn* (Universal) has been called a Western version of *The African Queen* because the relationship between Wayne and Katharine Hepburn is similar to that experienced by Hepburn and Humphrey Bogart in the older film. Director: Stuart Millar.

117. Ruth Roland.

118. Second from the right, manhandling the man with the rifle. Director: Robert F. Hill.

119. James Fenimore Cooper's *The Last of the Mohicans* featured Hobart Bosworth (left, as Chingachgook), Bob Kortman (with hatchet), Harry Carey (as Hawkeye) and Walter McGrail (right). Directors: B. Reeves Eason and Ford Beebe.

120. *Mystery Mountain* (Mascot, 1934; directed by Otto Brower and B. Reeves Eason.)

121. *The Phantom Empire* (Mascot, 1935; directed by Otto Brower and B. Reeves Eason) had Gene Autry in the underground city of Murania.

122. *The Miracle Rider* (Mascot, 1935; directed by Armand Schaefer and B. Reeves Eason). Also pictured: Chief Big Tree, Artie Ortego, Bob Kortman, Edward Earle.

123. John Carroll in *Zorro Rides Again* (Republic, 1937; directed by William Witney and John English), based on the character created by Johnston McCulley.

124. Top row: George Letz (later George Montgomery) and Lane Chandler. Bottom row: Lee Powell (the real Masked Man), Herman Brix (later Bruce Bennett) and Hal Taliaferro (formerly Wally Wales). Directors: William Witney and John English.

125. Gordon Elliott became Bill Elliott after starring in *The Great Adventures of Wild Bill Hickok* (Columbia, 1938). He's seen here with Hal Taliaferro and Richard Fiske. Directors: Sam Nelson and Norman Deming.

126. *The Adventures of Red Ryder* starred Don "Red" Barry, previously and subsequently known as Donald Barry. The badmen are Bill Wilkus and Frankie Marvin. Directors: William Witney and John English.

127. Leo Carrillo and Buck Jones, here, starred with Dick Foran, Charles Bickford, Lon Chaney, Jr., Noah Beery, Jr., Guinn "Big Boy" Williams and Monte Blue. Leading lady Jeanne Kelly later became Jean Brooks. Directors: Ford Beebe and Ray Taylor.

128. George J. Lewis (left) and Chief (Tonto) Thundercloud. Director: B. Reeves Eason.

129. George J. Lewis and Linda Stirling. She played The Whip (never called Zorro), but he put on the costume to help her. Directors: Spencer Gordon Bennet and Wallace Grissell.

130. None, probably, except to a real film buff. Their names are Harold Goodwin (a veteran of silent films), Peter Cookson and Victoria Horne. Directors: Ray Taylor and Lewis D. Collins.

131. Armida. Director: Michael Curtiz.

132. Frank Fay and George E. Stone.

133. Buddy Ebsen was featured. The songs were by Gus Kahn and Sigmund Romberg. Director: Robert Z. Leonard.

134. Guy Kibbee (left), Lionel Barrymore (seated) and Edward Arnold, who is manhandling Eddy. C. E. Anderson was the sheriff. Director: Jack Conway.

135. Penny Singleton in *Go West, Young Lady*. The men in the still are The Foursome (Gil Merchon, Del Porter, Ray Johnson and Dwight Snyder). Director: Frank R. Strayer.

136. Roy Rogers and Dale Evans wed in 1947, after his first wife's death, and are still happily married. Director: Frank McDonald.

137. Betty Hutton sang "I'm an Indian, Too" by Irving Berlin. Director: George Sidney.

138. *Fancy Pants* (Paramount, 1950; directed by George Marshall). There was also a silent *Ruggles of Red Gap* (Paramount, 1923) starring Edward Everett Horton.

139. *Red Garters*, with Rosemary Clooney. Director: George Marshall.

140. Van and Fosse, although they were at MGM around this time, were not in the film. The others are named in the order they appear in the still, except that Keel is in the middle. Director: Stanley Donen.

141. Jeanne Crain, Mamie Van Doren and Keith Andes. Director: George Marshall.

142. Shirley Jones and Gordon MacRae sang the immortal songs of Richard Rodgers and Oscar Hammerstein II. Director: Fred Zinnemann.

143. Harve Presnell in *The Unsinkable Molly Brown*. Director: Charles Walters.

144. Lee Marvin and Jean Seberg also starred, Joshua Logan directed.

145. Douglas MacLean, pictured with a girl, Muriel Frances Dana, who played a boy. Director: James W. Horne.

146. The title spoofed Zane Grey's *Riders of the Purple Sage*. Ralph Graves (center) and Vernon Dent (right) were featured. The big man was named Tiny Ward. Director: Ralph Cedar.

147. Margaret Livingston and Guinn "Big Boy" Williams. Director: James C. McKay.

148. The Baby Burlesk series, starring Shirley Temple. Director: Charles Lamont.

149. Oliver Hardy and Stan Laurel cavorted in *Way Out West* (MGM, 1936; directed by James W. Horne).

150. Cecilia Parker was big sister to Mickey Rooney's Andy Hardy in *Out West with the Hardys* (MGM, 1938; directed by George B. Seitz.)

151. Jack Carson, Dennis O'Keefe, Buddy Ebsen, Virginia Dale, Iron Eyes Cody (Indian in the rear), Spencer Charters, Jack Perrin (previously a star in B Westerns). Director: S. Sylvan Simon.

152. Bud Abbott (looking upward) and Lou Costello (on the fence) starred with Johnny Mack Brown in *Ride 'Em Cowboy*. Director: Arthur Lubin.

153. Yvonne De Carlo and Rod Cameron in *Frontier Gal*. Director: Charles Lamont.

154. Eve Arden, ogling Gale Storm and Donald O'Connor. Director: Charles Lamont.

155. *Callaway Went Thataway*, with Dorothy McGuire and Howard Keel (as Callaway and his double). Directors: Norman Panama and Melvin Frank.

156. *The First Traveling Saleslady*, with Barry Nelson. Director: Arthur Lubin.

157. Wendell Corey (left) was Jesse in *Alias Jesse James*. Director: Norman McLeod.

158. Ernie Kovacs, Stewart Granger and Fabian. British-born Granger starred in several Hollywood oaters, later appearing in foreign-made sagebrushers. Director: Henry Hathaway.

159. *The Second Time Around* (20th, 1961; directed by Vincent Sherman), with Andy Griffith and Thelma Ritter.

160. Melvyn Douglas, Stella Stevens, Joan Blondell and Glenn Ford.

161. *The Rounders*, directed by Burt Kennedy.

162. Joey Bishop, Dean Martin and Alain Delon. Director: Michael Gordon.

163. James Garner and Vera Miles. Director: Bernard McEveety.

164. Because they really are wood. Decoys were set up by the good people to fool the raiders. Director: Mel Brooks.

165. Franco Nero, Lynn Redgrave and American-born Eli Wallach. Director: Duccio Tessari.

166. Sam Waterston, playing an Indian, and Jeff Bridges.

167. William (Stage) Boyd (not to be confused with the William Boyd who played Hopalong Cassidy) and Gary Cooper clashed in *The Spoilers* (Paramount, 1930; directed by Edwin Carewe).

168. Cecil B. DeMille directed, Lupe Velez and Warner Baxter co-starred.

169. *Destry Rides Again* (Universal, 1939; directed by George Marshall), previously made with Tom Mix, had Dietrich fighting Una Merkel. Dietrich was killed at the end, protecting the man she loved, in this case James Stewart.

170. Mary Howard in the 1941 MGM version of *Billy the Kid*, directed by David Miller.

171. Richard Barthelmess in another version of *The Spoilers*. Director: Ray Enright.

172. Barbara Britton is the lady. The line is, "When you want to call me that, smile," or words to that effect. The film is *The Virginian*. Director: Stuart Gilmore.

173. Shelley played the title role of *Frenchie* (Universal, 1950; directed by Louis King) and fought Marie Windsor.

174. Anne Baxter. The Oklahoma land rush of 1889 was a highlight. Director: Anthony Mann.

175. Rex Lease, later a character actor. Also facing the camera: Blackjack Ward, little Bobby Nelson, Blackie Whiteford. Director: Elmer Clifton.

176. Robert, or Bob, Allen. He still can be seen in TV commercials. Director: Spencer Gordon Bennet.

177. Charles Starrett, later The Durango Kid. Director: Folmer Blangsted.

178. It's Gene Autry, flanked by Judith Allen and Lester (Smiley) Burnette. Director: Joseph Kane.

179. Roy Rogers and Julie Bishop. Stuntman Henry Wills is at the left. Director: Joseph Kane.

180. Bob Baker, previously a star at Universal, co-starred with Johnny Mack Brown (right). The girl is Frances Robinson, her dad being played by Frank LaRue. Director: Ray Taylor.

181. Jack Randall (brother of Bob Livingston) and Glenn Strange. Director: Raymond K. Johnson.

182. Andy Clyde (California Carlson), William Boyd (the original and only Hoppy), Russell Hayden (Lucky Jenkins). Director: Derwin M. Abrahams.

183. Tim McCoy and Charles King, a villain supreme. Ed Brady is surveying the scene with disbelief. Director: Spencer Gordon Bennet.

184. Tom Tyler, Jimmy Dodd and Bob Steele. Director: John English.

185. Rex Bell (Clara Bow's husband) and Mona Barrie. Director: Howard Bretherton.

186. Buster Crabbe continued his "Billy the Kid" series merely by changing his name to Billy Carson. Director of *The Drifter:* Sam Newfield.

187. Don "Red" Barry, here with Jack O'Shea, Frank McCarroll, Bob Kortman, Ernie Adams and Kenne Duncan. Director: Howard Bretherton.

188. Bob Livingston, brother of Jack Randall, seen here with Kenne Duncan and Cliff Parkinson. Director: Spencer Gordon Bennet.

189. Monte Hale, with Sunset Carson. Director: Thomas Carr.

190. Eddie Dean and Jennifer Holt (daughter of Jack). Director: Ray Taylor.

191. Gilbert Roland. Director: William Nigh.

192. Allan "Rocky" Lane was Red, and Bobby (now Robert) Blake played Little Beaver. Director: R. G. Springsteen.

193. Lash LaRue, who later made *Hard on the Trail* (1971), here bringing to justice Lane Bradford, son of veteran badman John Merton. Director: Ray Taylor.

194. Whip Wilson and Andy Clyde. Director: Ray Taylor.

195. Tim Holt and Movita. Director: Lesley Selander.

196. Starrett was The Durango Kid; Clayton Moore won fame as The Lone Ranger of features and TV. Director: Ray Nazarro.

197. James Ellison and Russell Hayden, here in *Hostile Country*. Director: Thomas Carr.

198. Rex Allen, who made his debut in *The Arizona Cowboy* (1950), vanquishing Roy Barcroft. Director: William Witney.

199. *The Oklahoma Kid* (Warners, 1939), directed by Lloyd Bacon. Also featured: (left) Trevor Bardette, Ward Bond and Ray Mayer.

200. Clark Gable and Lana Turner in *Honky Tonk* (MGM, 1941; directed by Jack Conway).

201. *The Sea of Grass* (MGM, 1947), directed by Elia Kazan, had Harry Carey in one of his last roles.

202. *Branded* (Paramount, 1950; directed by Rudolph Mate) also starred Mona Freeman (left), Selena Royle and Charles Bickford.

203. *Rancho Notorious*, directed by Fritz Lang, co-starred Arthur Kennedy (left) and Mel Ferrer (whom Dietrich is touching). Others: John Kellogg, Lloyd Gough, the now better-known Jack Elam, Dan Seymour.

204. Barbara Stanwyck and Fred MacMurray in one of the few black-and-white 3-Dimensional Westerns. Director: Roy Rowland.

205. *River of No Return*, directed by Otto Preminger, with Rory Calhoun (center) and young Tommy Rettig.

206. Crawford met Mercedes McCambridge in the final showdown. Sterling Hayden played Johnny. Director: Nicholas Ray.

207. Burt Lancaster was Wyatt Earp, Kirk Douglas played Doc Holliday. Director: John Sturges.

208. Marlon Brando.

209. *How the West Was Won* (MGM, 1963), directed by John Ford, Henry Hathaway and George Marshall.

210. *Shenandoah* (Universal, 1965; directed by Andrew V. McLaglen), with Katharine Ross and James Stewart.

211. *Bandolero!* (20th Century-Fox, 1968). Director: Andrew V. McLaglen.

212. *Hang 'Em High* (UA, 1968; directed by Ted Post).

213. *Dirty Dingus Magee* (MGM, 1970; directed by Burt Kennedy), with Michele Carey.

214. Toshiro Mifune and Charles Bronson. Director: Terence Young.

215. *Joe Kidd*, directed by John Sturges for Universal in 1972.

216. *The Revengers* (National General, 1972; directed by Daniel Mann), the last film of Susan Hayward, starred William Holden. Ironically, she replaced Mary Ure, who died about the same time as Miss Hayward. Van Heflin signed to do the role played by Ernest Borgnine and died before filming began.

217. Mae Clarke, of *The Public Enemy*, and Ralph (Ellery Queen, President Roosevelt) Bellamy. Director: Howard Bretherton.

218. Rita Hayworth and Western star Tom Keene. Director: Lynn Shores.

219. Robert Cummings and Joan Bennett. Character actress May Robson is the elderly lady on the wagon. Director: James Hogan.

220. Jennifer Jones, here acting under her real name of Phylis Isley. Director: George Sherman.

221. Kay Francis and Mary Gordon. Director: George Marshall.

222. Ann Miller, George "Gabby" Hayes and Mary Lee. Director: Joseph Santley.

223. Hugh Herbert and Frances Farmer. Director: Alfred E. Green.

224. William Bishop, and Mary Stuart of *Search For Tomorrow*. The only other star of the film, incidentally, was Preston Foster, the title role being played by a horse. Director: Phil Karlson.

225. Paul Fix and ZaSu Pitts. Director: Byron Haskin.

226. Vaughn Monroe, with Jean Parker and, at left, Victor Jory and Edgar Buchanan. Director: R. G. Springsteen.

227. *The Violent Men* (Columbia, 1955; directed by Rudolph Mate), with Glenn Ford and Barbara Stanwyck.

228. Robert Clarke, Andrea King and Harry James. Director: Herbert S. Greene.

229. Jo Van Fleet and John Ireland. The bartender is Paul Bradley. Director: John Sturges.

230. Marty Robbins. The boy is Michael David. Director: Bill Ward.

231. Barbara Hershey (Seagull) and Carolyn Jones. As an Indian girl, Ms. Hershey was cast opposite David Carradine, with whom she later became romantically involved. Director: Lee H. Katzin.

232. Ida Lupino, with McQueen, Joe Don Baker, and Robert Preston (back to camera) as her husband.

Index of Performers

*Only those performers actually shown in the stills are indexed. The numbers are those of the stills (stills **A** through **F** appear on the covers).*

Index of Films

*Only the films for which there are stills are indexed. The numbers are those of the stills (stills **A** through **F** appear on the covers).*